AIRCRAFT

CONTENTS

CONTENTS

This is a Grandreams Book
This edition published in 2004

Grandreams Books Ltd
4 North Parade, Bath BA1 1LF, UK

Designed and packaged by
Q2A Design Studio

Printed in China

FLYING FIRSTS

From fabled Chinese princes and their flying chariots, to the mythical flying carpets of Persia, history and legend are full of tales about people who tried to reach up to the skies. Indeed, one of man's earliest dreams was to fly!

Early Birds

In 1670, an Italian monk, in his attempt to create a balloon, designed a strange machine – four air-filled spheres attached to a boat! The first successful balloon was flown only a century later by the Montgolfier Brothers.

Various other ideas for lightweight balloons and flying machines followed, but it was Sir George Cayley, an Englishman, who changed the course of flight history. Starting with motor gliders, Cayley built all kinds of machines to test his ideas for making heavier-than-air objects fly. He was the first man to study the scientific principles of flight.

Flying High

The first successfull aeroplane was the Wright Brothers' *Flyer* of 1903. It was made of cloth and paper. Today, aeroplanes, helicopters, gliders and other lightweight aircraft have made travelling around the world possible and, indeed, easy.

Sir Geroge Cayley

FLYING FIRSTS

The Montgolfier Balloon in flight

The Hindenburg

Which was the first air crash to be recorded on camera?

The *Hindenberg*, a huge German zeppelin, burst into flames while landing in New Jersey, U.S., in 1937. The tragedy was taped by press reporters present at the airport.

When was the first commercial air service established?

In 1910, Count Ferdinand von Zeppelin of Germany started the first commercial air service between Europe and America. The airships were called 'zeppelins'.

Who launched the first hot-air balloon?

In November 1783, Etienne and Joseph Montgolfier, wealthy paper merchants, launched the first hot-air balloon. Pieces of straw and bits of wool were burnt as fuel to sustain the flight.

Why did George Cayley's Aerial Carriage never take off?

The Aerial Carriage could not be tested because George Cayley could not find the right engine for it! The 1843 convertiplane combined the concepts of an aeroplane and a helicopter and had four rotors resembling the wheels of a carriage.

Sir George Cayley's Aerial Carriage

What was the inspiration behind Sir George Cayley's glider?

An ordinary kite inspired Sir George Cayley to invent the glider. His first glider had a movable tail and was mounted on wooden sticks.

What was special about the 1913 *Sikorsky Bolshoi* airliner?

The *Sikorsky Bolshoi* airliner of 1913 was the first four-engine aircraft to fly. Besides being the largest aircraft at the time, it was also the first to have a large passenger cabin.

Who made the first successful flight across the English Channel?

French pilot Louis Bleriot made the first flight across the English Channel in 1909. The flight won Bleriot a prize of £1,000. The aircraft used by him came to be known as *Cross-Channel Bleriot XI*.

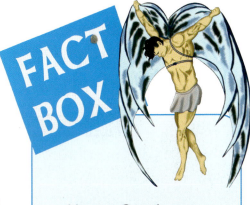

☐ Harriet Quimby was the first licensed female pilot in America. In 1912, she also became the first woman to fly across the English Channel.

☐ In 1924, two Douglas World Cruisers (DWC), taking off from Seattle, Washington, made the first around-the-world flight. The expedition was completed in 175 days.

☐ Sir George Cayley, known as the 'Father of Aerial Navigation', was the first to think about vertical flight (elevation). In 1799, he designed the first aeroplane with wings, a fuselage, a tail unit and a mechanism that made vertical flight possible.

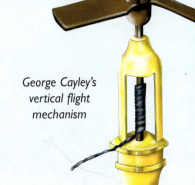

George Cayley's vertical flight mechanism

FLYING FIRSTS

How did the French inventor Besnier experiment with flying?

Besnier first attached four huge panels on to levers, which he rested on his shoulders. In imitation of a bird in flight, he moved the levers with his hands and feet, reaching the ground from the top of a house!

Besnier and his strange flying machine

Who was the first woman to fly a supersonic plane?

In 1953, Jacqueline Cochran, an American pilot, became the first woman to fly faster than the speed of sound (supersonic speed). At the time of her death in 1980, she held more speed, altitude and distance records than any other pilot in history.

What is the 'Flyer'?

The first heavier-than-air aircraft made by the Wright brothers is called the *Flyer*. Orville Wright had first flown it on December 17, 1903, at the Kill Devil Hills in North Carolina, U.S., for 12 seconds. The aircraft is now housed at the Smithsonian Institution in Washington, D.C.

Who was the first woman to fly solo across the Atlantic?

American aviator Amelia Earhart flew solo across the Atlantic in 1932. In 1937 she set out for an around-the-world flight. However, more than halfway into her journey, her plane mysteriously vanished.

Which was the world's first jet airliner to enter regular passenger service?

The *De Havilland Comet* - flying from London to Johannesburg on May 2, 1952 - was the world's first jet airliner to enter regular passenger service.

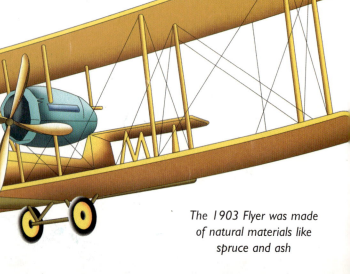

The 1903 Flyer was made of natural materials like spruce and ash

TYPES OF AIRCRAFT

The dream of flying spurred people to invent many different forms of air machines.

At First...

Gliders were the first aircraft with wings. Airships were very popular in the early 1900s.

Hovering Helis

Helicopters score over other aircraft for their ability to move in all directions. They can even hover in mid-air! The first successful helicopter dates back to 1936.

Unlimited Uses

Passenger liners and private jets carry millions across the world everyday. Air forces have extremely sophisticated aircraft to protect their nations. Other aircraft include cargo planes, seaplanes, supersonic jets and even flying cars! There are smaller, lighter and easy-to-fly aircraft that many people fly for fun.

The microlight is a lightweight plane developed in the 1970s from hang-gliders

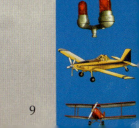

TYPES OF AIRCRAFT

The first aeroplane to fly was a biplane

Triplanes were found to be more powerful than biplanes because of an extra pair of wings

What is the difference between biplanes and triplanes?

Triplanes have three wings, one above the other, while biplanes only have two. The extra wing gives triplanes greater moving and lifting power. These were used as fighter planes during World War I (1914-18).

Why were biplanes considered better than monoplanes?

Unlike monoplanes, biplanes have two sets of wings, one placed above the other and supported by wires. In the early 20th century, the biplane was considered stronger than the monoplane.

What is the difference between the terms 'aircraft' and 'aeroplane'?

The term 'aircraft' refers to all flying machines, including aeroplanes, helicopters and hot-air balloons. Aircraft may range from simple hang-gliders to the enormous jumbo jets. The 'aeroplane', on the other hand, is a powered, heavier-than-air aircraft with fixed wings.

What is a monoplane?

A narrow aeroplane with a single set of supporting wings is called a monoplane. Louis Bleriot's *Cross-Channel Bleriot XI* was a monoplane. Most modern aeroplanes are monoplanes too.

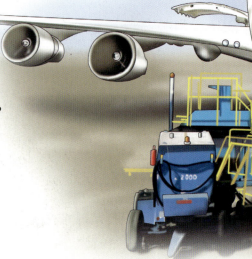

A cargo plane

What are airships commonly used for?

The earliest use of airships was to carry people from one place to another. This helium-filled aircraft was soon replaced with more sophisticated aeroplanes for passenger service. Airships are now mainly used for advertising or taking aerial photographs.

What is the function of observation planes?

Observation planes are usually standard light aircraft. These are used by the police or the army for investigation purposes. Rescue services also use observation planes to locate victims after a mishap, or to study the location of the mishap.

How do cargo planes carry goods from one place to another?

Cargo aeroplanes are designed to transport all types of goods, such as parcels, military weapons, animals, vehicles and even other small aircraft. These goods are usually stored in the sides of the plane. Some planes, like the Boeing 747-400, have noses that can open up for storing large cargo.

FACT BOX

□ Lightweight aircraft with small engines are called ultralights. They are usually home-built, inexpensive and easy to fly.

□ The Boeing Company is the world's biggest manufacturer of commercial aircraft. The American company is said to have built more than 14,000 jetliners.

□ The Boeing 747, or the 'jumbo jet', is the world's largest passenger aeroplane. The first prototype of this large aircraft was rolled out in 1968. Powered with a jet engine, the plane can carry over 400 passengers.

The Boeing 747 passenger liner

TYPES OF AIRCRAFT

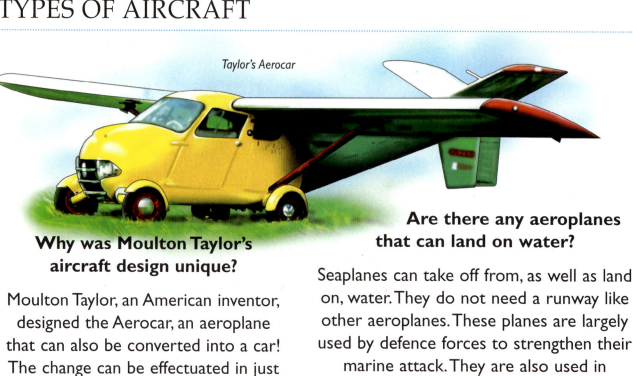

Taylor's Aerocar

Why was Moulton Taylor's aircraft design unique?

Moulton Taylor, an American inventor, designed the Aerocar, an aeroplane that can also be converted into a car! The change can be effectuated in just about 15 minutes. The wings can be folded back along its sides.

Are all jet aircraft supersonic?

Supersonic planes are only those jet aircraft that can travel faster than the speed of sound. Their shape is different from that of conventional aeroplanes. They also require large quantities of fuel to sustain their high-powered flight.

Are there any aeroplanes that can land on water?

Seaplanes can take off from, as well as land on, water. They do not need a runway like other aeroplanes. These planes are largely used by defence forces to strengthen their marine attack. They are also used in remote areas such as Northern Canada and Alaska, which have few airfields.

What advantage do propellered planes have over jet aircraft?

Propellered planes have propellers that are driven by gas turbines. As a result, these planes are cheaper to run than jet aircraft. They can also take off easily from short runways. However, these planes are unsuitable for travelling long distances.

Why are tiltrotor aeroplanes so called?

A tiltrotor plane's engines and propellers tilt in different directions to fly. The rotors are tilted upward for vertical flight and forward for fast, forward movement.

Tiltrotors combine the best functional features of aeroplanes and helicopters

WAR CRY!

Fighter planes, bombers, spy planes and observation aircraft play an important role during wars between nations.

Not a Smooth Start, but....

In September 1908, in order to test the famous *Flyer*, American Lieutenant Thomas Selfridge went on a flight with Orville Wright. Unfortunately, the propeller broke and the plane crashed. However, it was the Wright Brothers who, in 1909, finally built the world's first military aeroplane.

The World Wars

The World Wars greatly changed the way military planes were used. From being merely tools for observation, they were modfied for use in bombing and air attacks. Dutchman Anthony Fokker designed a system for firing a machine gun through an aircraft's propeller. The British BE2 was one of the first aircraft to drop bombs.

With World War II came the era of jet-propelled aircraft and faster, more powerful warplanes. The fabric-covered biplanes were displaced by metal-bodied monoplanes.

The Sopwith Pup was the first British fighter designed to fire through the propeller

WAR CRY!

What are fighter planes used for?

The fastest of all warplanes, fighters are designed to win air superiority so that other slower aircraft, like observers and bombers, can operate over battle zones. Fighters carry out ground attacks as well as assaults on enemy fighter planes. The Russian MiG-25 is one of the fastest fighter aircraft in service.

A bomber plane

Which country owns the Northrop B-2 Stealth Bomber?

The United States owns the Northrop B-2 Stealth Bomber. This warplane is designed to absorb or deflect enemy radar, so that it can remain undetected while approaching its targets.

The Stealth Bomber is protected by its shape

What kind of weapons do fighter planes use to attack enemy aircraft?

Fighter planes use a variety of missiles, torpedoes, machine guns and bombs to fire at enemies. One such weapon is the air-to-air AIM-9 Sidewinder missile. It is classified as a smart weapon because it has an in-built system that allows it to home in on its target.

What role do aircraft usually play in a war?

There are a variety of aircraft specially designed for war. They are equipped with sophisticated electronic instruments. Their role in a war ranges from detecting and attacking enemy targets, to supplying weapons to other aircraft. Some aircraft are also used for carrying troops from one battle zone to another.

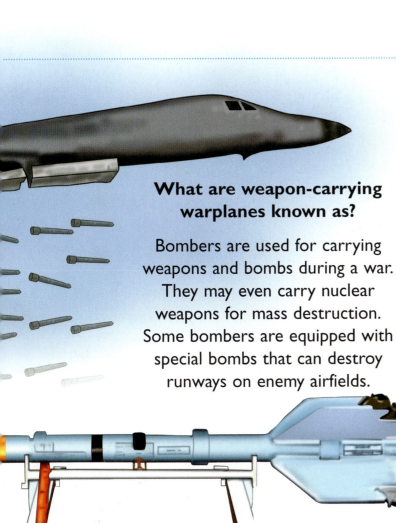

What are weapon-carrying warplanes known as?

Bombers are used for carrying weapons and bombs during a war. They may even carry nuclear weapons for mass destruction. Some bombers are equipped with special bombs that can destroy runways on enemy airfields.

Sidewinder AIM-9 missile

How effective are helicopters as war aircraft?

Helicopters are used to move troops and equipment rapidly into battle zones. Heavily armed helicopters called helicopter gunships are widely used during war. These are equipped with rapid-fire machine guns that fire from the turret.

Are there special planes for observing and reporting the movement of enemy forces?

Aerial Reconnaissance Planes, or observation planes, are airborne observers that report the movement of enemy forces. These planes are a prime target for enemy fighters. Observation planes are usually pilotless and remote-controlled.

WAR CRY!

How do wings help fighter planes to fly faster and evade enemy attacks in the air?

Some military aeroplanes, like the F-14 Tomcat fighter, are equipped with 'swing wings'. These wings are fully spread out during take-off, but, once in the air, they can fully swing to the back of the aircraft. This not only helps the aeroplane to fly faster, but also allows it to dodge low-flying enemy aircraft.

How many people does the aircrew of a fighter plane consist of?

The term 'aircrew' includes the flying crew and the ground crew. A fighter plane usually carries a two-member crew - the pilot and the weapon-systems operator. The pilot carries flight plans in his knee pads.

What kind of a warplane is the Harrier?

British Aerospace's Harrier, or the 'jump jet', is a V/STOL aircraft. It can fly up or down, sideways or backwards and can even hover like a helicopter. Its wheels fold up into the wings during a flight. The 'jump jet' is a very useful warplane because it can take off or land almost anywhere.

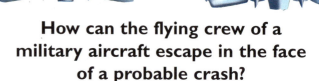

The 'swing wings' of the F-14 Tomcat fighter make the plane flexible

How can the flying crew of a military aircraft escape in the face of a probable crash?

Most military aircraft have ejector seats that shoot the crew out to safety. In an emergency, the crew members pull a handle that releases the cockpit canopy. They are then shot out of the aircraft along with their seats. As a person drops to a particular height, the seat falls away and a parachute opens up to see him through to a safe landing.

Which fighter aeroplane was the first to set records for speed, climbing speed and height?

The F-104 (Starfighter) was the first fighter aeroplane to set world records for speed, ascending speed and height. The aircraft is built with short wingspans, making it a lightweight. In fact, the F-104 Starfighter is so light, it is sometimes called the 'missile with a man in it!'

The F-104 (Starfighter)

THE METALLIC BIRD

The earliest experiments in flying were not very successful. These were done with air-filled bags and hand-movable flaps, which were good enough only for a short stay in mid-air. The early inventors did not fully understand the basic science of flying.

Aerodynamics

Aerodynamics is the study of air in motion. The name originated from the Greek words 'aer', meaning air and 'dynamis', which means power. It is this science that makes it possible for aircraft to fly. Aerodynamics observes the forces that act on solid objects moving in air and how the air acts upon an aircraft's aerofoil (wing).

Four Forces

There are four forces that act on an aeroplane in flight - lift, weight, thrust and drag. Weight refers to the force of gravity on the aircraft. Lift is the upward force that balances the aircraft's weight. Thrust is the forward push of the aircraft. Drag is the force of air that slows down forward movement.

An aeroplane can fly only when its lift is greater than its weight and when the thrust of its engines is greater than the drag of the air

THE METALLIC BIRD

Why do aeroplanes have a streamlined body?

Streamlining cuts down drag, or air resistance, by helping air to flow smoothly past an object. Teardrop-shaped objects such as aerofoils are streamlined for this reason. The lesser the drag, the better the movement of the aeroplane.

How do aerofoils affect the airflow around an aeroplane?

The upper surface of an aerofoil is longer - and more curved - than its lower surface. The air flowing over the aerofoil has to travel farther than the air below. In order to keep up with the speed of the air flowing below, the air above the aerofoil ends up travelling faster. Thus, the airflow above the aeroplane wings is much faster.

Fuselage

Pilot's seat

Elevator

What does the term 'airframe' stand for?

The fuselage (the central body portion), wings, tailplane and tailfin are together called the airframe of an aeroplane. These make up the main stuctural features of an aeroplane. While the fuselage lends weight to the aircraft, the wings carry it into air and the tail keeps it steady.

Flap

Ailerons to steer the plane

Wings are made from iron rods

The fundamental parts of an aircraft

What made the *Flyer* a success despite its not having a streamlined body?

The *Flyer* was a biplane that did not have a streamlined body. However, drag increases only with speed and the *Flyer* did not fly fast enough to make streamlining necessary.

How heavy are the wings of an aeroplane?

An aeroplane's wings are not solid, but hollow. A thin skin of lightweight material covers the aerofoil structure supported by the girder-shaped wing beam. This makes the wings strong, but as light as possible.

How do swing wings contribute to an aeroplane's speed and lift?

During take-off and landing, moveable swing wings are stretched out for good lift. During a flight, however, these are swept back in order to reduce drag and increase speed. Modern jets like Panavia Tornado Adv, 1984, have moveable swing wings.

How do the flaps and slats on aeroplane wings work?

Aeroplane wings are equipped with flaps and slats for achieving extra lift. By extending the size of the wings and the curve of the aerofoils, they spread out the airflow over a larger area. These features also facilitate swift take-offs and slow, smooth landings. Flaps are located on the trailing edges of the wings, while slats are situated on the leading edges of the engine.

Fuel tank

Spinner

Propeller

Aeroplane wings have slats and flaps that help in flight. Flaps increase the wing size, which gives the aircraft more lift for take-off. Slats help to reduce lift before an aircraft lands

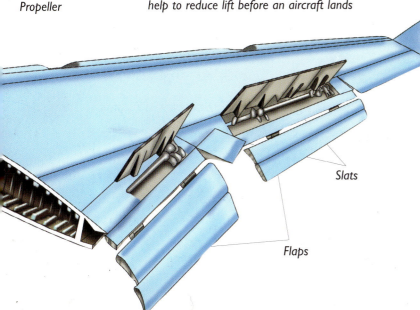

Slats

Flaps

FACT BOX

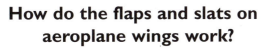

Propellers are driven by the aeroplane's engine. They thrust the aeroplane forwards just as the wings lift it upwards

❑ Propellers, or airscrews, are fan-like objects fixed either on the aeroplane's nose, or on each of the wings. As a propeller turns, its blades pull in air from the front and push it out to the back.

❑ The pointed nose of Concorde helps the aeroplane to fly at great speed. However, during take-offs and landings, the nose blocks the pilot's view. Hence, the nose has an instrument that allows it to 'droop' down, away from the pilot's view!

❑ Gliders have special air brakes on their wings that help the aircraft to descend quickly and smoothly for landing.

THE METALLIC BIRD

Why are aeroplane tyres filled with nitrogen gas?

Aeroplane tyres are filled with nitrogen because it is an incombustible gas, i.e., it does not burn. During take-offs and landings, the tyres can rub the ground so hard that they may generate enough heat to catch fire.

The front gear tyre of an aeroplane

What is the role of the aeroplane's rudder?

The rudder of an aeroplane helps to steer the plane in flight. It is situated in the tail section.

The jet engine of an aeroplane

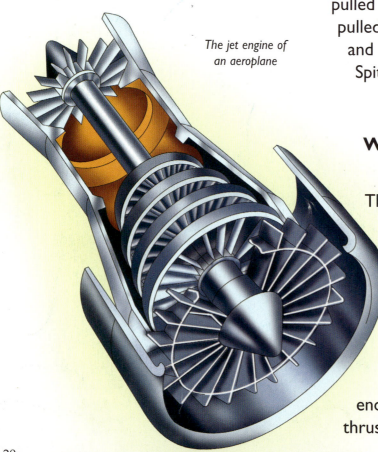

Why do most aeroplanes require a runway almost 1,500 m (4,921 feet) long?

Winged aircraft can fly only when there is enough lift to overcome their weight. Lift is the upward force that pushes aircraft into air. It is created when air pressure over the wings decreases. Air pressure, in turn, decreases with speed. Aeroplanes move along the runway to keep air flowing past their wings, with the flow much faster above than below. This helps create the required lift.

Why do some warplanes have retractable main wheels?

Some warplanes, like the Supermarine Spitfire of 1936, have wheels that can be pulled up during a flight. As the wheels are pulled out of the airflow, drag is reduced and speed increases. The Supermarine Spitfire became famous as a combat machine during World War II.

What kind of engines do the fastest aeroplanes have?

The fastest aeroplanes are equipped with jet engines. These engines suck air in at one end and force it out of the other at a much greater speed. This action thrusts the aircraft in the opposite direction. The engine burns fuel and pushes exhaust gases out from the back at enormous speed. This backward push thrusts the aeroplane forward quickly.

FLYING AN AEROPLANE

Each part of an aeroplane – the fuselage, wings, undercarriage (landing gear) and tail assembly – is vital to flight. The airframe of an aeroplane refers to the basic plane.

Tail Talk

A very important feature of an aeroplane is the tail assembly. It is the stabilising force that controls the aircraft's swing. It is also used for the pitching and yawing actions.

The tail assembly is made up of a horizontal stabiliser and elevators and a vertical fin and rudder. The stabiliser keeps the aircraft steady during flight and prevent the plane's nose from swinging sideways (i.e., yawing). They also safeguard the nose against up-and-down fluctuations (i.e., pitching).

Tail Types

The tail assemblies come in an array of designs, each useful for different kinds of movements. Some common ones include right-angle assembly, swept-back assembly, T-assembly, anhedral assembly, V-assembly and twin assembly. The V-assembly, also known as the Butterfly, is preferred for lighter planes. Most jet engines, on the other hand, use the T-assembly.

The tail assembly of an aeroplane is also called empennage

FLYING AN AEROPLANE

What are the main kinds of movements made by an aeroplane in flight?

The main movements made by an aeroplane in flight are rolling, pitching and yawing. Moving the rudder in a specific direction turns the nose of the aeroplane in that direction. This helps the aeroplane take a turn while flying.

Do passenger airliners need multiple engines?

Passenger airliners show great variety in the number and position of their engines. While some airliners have four engines (two mounted on each of their wings), the others have three engines distributed between their wings and the tail. All airliners are designed in such a way that they are able to land safely on just one engine, should the others fail.

What is 'rolling'?

The ailerons on the two wings of an aeroplane are joined to each other by wires. When one aileron goes up, the other goes down. This causes one wing to rise and the other to drop, making the aircraft tilt to one side. This change of position of the aeroplane is called 'rolling' or 'banking'.

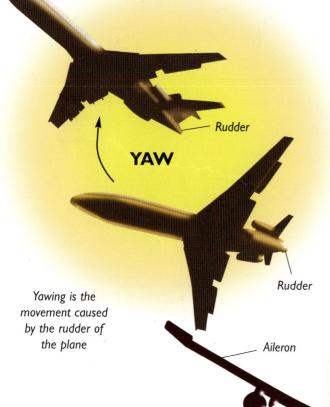

Rudder

YAW

Rudder

Aileron

Yawing is the movement caused by the rudder of the plane

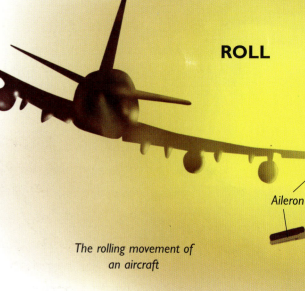

ROLL

Aileron

The rolling movement of an aircraft

What are control surfaces?

All aeroplanes have moveable parts on their wings and tail. The moveable parts on the wings are the ailerons and those on the tail are the elevators and the rudder. Together, they are known as control surfaces. They are used to change the direction of the flow of air, so that the aeroplane can turn or tilt in flight.

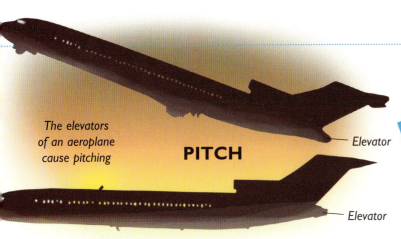

The elevators of an aeroplane cause pitching

PITCH

Elevator

Elevator

What is 'pitching'?

The action of elevators on the movement of an aeroplane is called 'pitching'. When the elevators are raised, the nose of the plane points upwards and its tail dips down. Thus, the aeroplane is said to be pitched upwards as it gains altitude after take-off.

How are the control surfaces operated to turn or tilt the aeroplane?

In most aeroplanes, the control surfaces are moved hydraulically - i.e., through the pressure exerted by an oily fluid pumped along pipes. In modern 'fly-by-wire' aircraft, such as the Airbus A320, complex computer systems operate the controls. In the earliest models, however, the control surfaces had to be physically monitored by the pilot.

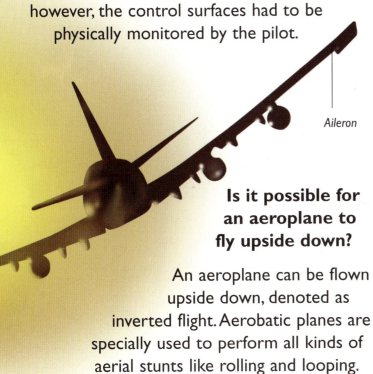

Aileron

Is it possible for an aeroplane to fly upside down?

An aeroplane can be flown upside down, denoted as inverted flight. Aerobatic planes are specially used to perform all kinds of aerial stunts like rolling and looping.

FACT BOX

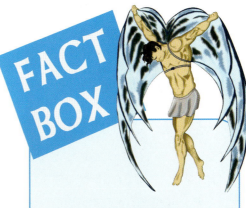

▫ An aeroplane's yoke moves the plane in the same way as a steering wheel moves a car. When the yoke is pulled back, the plane moves up; if pushed forward, the plane goes down.

▫ Lincoln Beachey, regarded as the 'father of aerobatic flying', became the first American, in 1913, to perform the 'loop the loop' stunt in his aeroplane *Curtiss*.

▫ Aeroplanes often bump up and down in flight. This is known as turbulence and is caused by the layers of atmospheric air constantly moving up and down. Just as boats bounce along the ocean's waves, aeroplanes, too, ride the layers of air in the sky.

FLYING AN AEROPLANE

Ernst Mach

What is the Mach number of an aircraft?

The Mach number for an aircraft is the measurement of its speed in terms of the speed of sound. It is named after the Austrian scientist, Ernest Mach, who worked it out. The number is calculated by dividing the aircraft's speed by the speed of sound. Thus, Mach 1 is the speed of sound (1,060 km/h) and Mach 2 is twice the speed of sound.

What type of engines do gliders use?

Gliders are non-powered aircraft and have no engines. They are pulled, or towed, for attaining gradual speed and lift. Either an aeroplane or a car tows the glider until the latter gets enough lift to glide in the air on its own!

What is a sonic boom?

When an aircraft flies faster than sound, the air in front of it gets compressed and forms a shock wave. The aircraft breaks through the shock wave, which travels right down and reaches the earth as a loud bang. This loud bang is known as a sonic boom.

What flight controls does a pilot use to fly an aeroplane?

A pilot flies his aeroplane by using various flight controls. These include the control stick, a pair of rudder pedals and a throttle lever. The throttle lever controls the engine power of the aeroplane.

How are the cabin lights and air conditioning of a plane powered when it is on the ground?

A small engine called the auxiliary power unit (APU) is used when the aeroplane is on ground and the main engines are switched off. The APU drives electrical generators to supply power for cabin lights and air conditioning as passengers board or get off the plane.

The throttle levers of an aeroplane

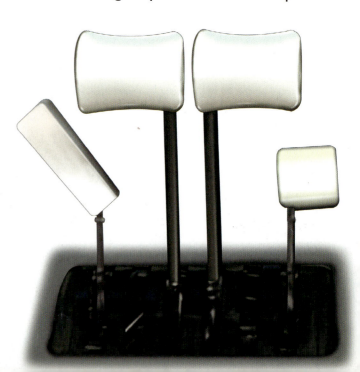

FINDING THE WAY

In the 1920s, as aeroplanes began to carry more and more people across longer distances, it became essential to set up air traffic systems to control and guide aircraft.

Radios and Radars

By the end of World War II, there were radio and radar networks to track several aircraft at a time. Radars reflect aircraft positions on display screens. Controllers can warn pilots of possibile collisions with other aircraft.

Light the Way

Earlier, aircraft did not fly very high and could be directed by hand signals. In the late 1930s, controllers started using light guns that sent out coloured light beams to aircraft. This system worked well for night flights too.

Safety in the Skies

Today, air traffic control is a vital part of all modern-day airports. Controllers keep track of all aircraft, from the time they taxi on the runway, to the take-off and landing stages.

Earlier, flags were waved to guide aircraft. Green-coloured flags meant pilots could go ahead with take-off or landing. Red flags directed pilots to wait for further instructions

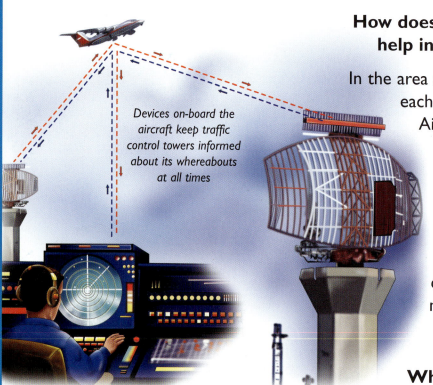

Devices on-board the aircraft keep traffic control towers informed about its whereabouts at all times

How does air traffic control (ATC) help in ensuring a safe flight?

In the area around and above an airport, each aircraft is guided by the ATC. Air traffic controllers speak to flight captains by radio. Information about each aircraft's height and position is collected by radar antennae at the airport and displayed on screens in the control tower. The controllers maintain a close watch on the path taken by the aircraft.

What is an air corridor?

An air corridor is a narrow, strip-like route that an aeroplane must fly along. Each aeroplane is assigned its own invisible air corridor by the air traffic control. No two aeroplanes have a common air corridor at a time. This keeps them away from each other and prevents mid-air collisions.

Do pilots plan the details of a flight before they take off?

Before a take-off, the captain of a flight must file a 'flight plan' with the air traffic control (ATC). The flight plan shows details of the route that the aeroplane will follow, along with the height and the speed at which it will fly. No aeroplane can take off without the approval of the flight plan by the ATC.

How do pilots on a flight know if they are keeping to their flight plan?

Ground-based radio transmitters, or radio beacons, emit radio signals that are caught by the radio system on an aeroplane. Pilots use the beacons as signposts to help them keep to their flight plan.

Can aeroplanes land without informing the air traffic control at the airport?

At the end of a flight, the flight captain radios the ATC to ask for permission to land. The controllers guide the aircrew to bring the aeroplane down safely. The engine power is reduced so that the aeroplane loses speed and height as it nears the runway.

How far apart are air corridors from one another?

Although air corridors criss-cross at certain places, there is a safe minimum distance that must be maintained between two aircraft. There must also be a minimum time gap of 10 minutes between two consecutive flights.

How do radar systems work?

A radar system works by sending out short bursts of radio signals. Like echoes, these signals bounce off any object they hit. The computers fitted in the aeroplane's flight deck record the time taken by the signals to bounce back and then calculate the distance between the object and the aircraft. This information is then displayed on a screen on the flight deck.

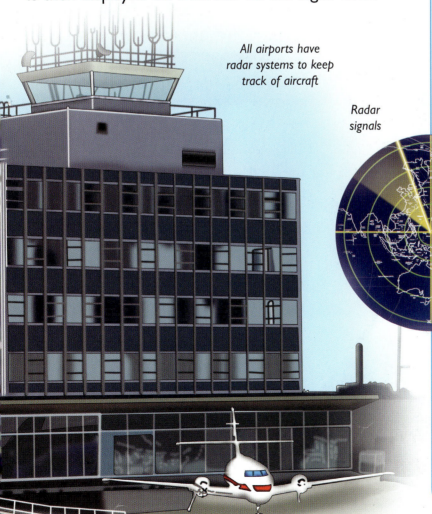

All airports have radar systems to keep track of aircraft

Radar signals

FACT BOX

❑ Pre-flight weather inspection informs pilots about imminent thunderstorms. Graphs, maps and radar reports show where and when storms are likely to occur. A weather radar device on-board the aeroplane can detect water, so the crew is forewarned about bad weather.

❑ Radar stands for 'radio detection and ranging'. Most planes have radar equipment in their nose cones. It cautions pilots about bad weather and objects they may fly into.

❑ Earlier, pilots used to find their way by looking out of the window for landmarks. Sometimes they even used automobile road maps! In 1919, Lieutenant Bruner, an American, started using bonfires to navigate planes at night.

FINDING THE WAY

What role do lighting systems play in flight safety?

Lighting systems are required both for night and day flights. All runways have lights positioned along the sides and in the middle. Rotating beacons on the top of control towers act like road traffic signals. Red-coloured obstruction warning lights are also provided to warn pilots of any danger ahead.

Obstruction warning lights

How are aircraft guided after landing?

After landing, the taxiing aircraft are guided by ground movement controllers to their parking positions in the hangar.

Ground traffic controller

How do air traffic controllers keep track of aircraft movements?

Air traffic controllers keep track of moving aeroplanes through radarscopes. Devices inside an aeroplane send signals to the radar reciever. These signals are then displayed on the radarscope. The tiny dots on the screen represent the aeroplanes in flight.

How do pilots find their way high up in the clouds without being able to see the ground at all?

Pilots and air traffic controllers use electronic systems to help them navigate. These systems transmit information beamed from radio equipment on the aeroplane, on the ground, and on satellites orbiting high above the earth.

Why do aeroplanes wait at the runway before take-off?

When an aeroplane is ready to leave, the captain radios the control tower for permission to start the engines. The aeroplane then taxies on to the runway, getting the engines to build up enough power to speed along the runway and take off.

AIRCRAFT TECHNOLOGY

Before the invention of powered flight, flying machines lacked engine power. In the 1920s, the unusual *Ca 60* was built with nine wings and eight engines! It crashed on its very first flight, soon after take-off.

Engine Count

Today, there are single-engine, twin-engine, three-engine and four-engine aircraft. Most modern aeroplanes have around three or four engines. Single-engine types are generally preferred for pilot training.

The number of engines vary across aircraft

Body Basics

The first flying machines were made of paper, linen, straw and other natural materials. Since then, aircraft technology has advanced tremendously. Now we have aircraft made of metals (like aluminium) and alloys (like steel). Those with non-metallic bodies - made of materials like Kevlar and carbon fibre - are much lighter and often much stronger too.

The Boeing 777 was the first aeroplane to be designed entirely on the computer. Some three million different parts were put together by means of 3-D computer graphics!

AIRCRAFT TECHNOLOGY

Is it possible for aircraft to be refuelled during a flight?

Aircraft tanks can be refuelled even while they are in flight. This is called air-to-air refuelling. A tanker aircraft extends a long hose, or a pole, to the aircraft it has to refuel. The pilot so aligns the plane that its tank connects with the end of the hose or pole.

Can computers fly aeroplanes on their own?

The autopilot is a computer device that can fly an aeroplane on its own. It is mostly used on long flights. However, a pilot is always present in the cockpit to keep an eye on the autopilot, to check if the flight is going according to plan.

How do pilots know the height at which they are flying the aircraft?

The cockpit has an instrument called the altimeter, which shows the height (above sea level) at which the aircraft is flying. It does so by measuring the air pressure outside the aircraft. Air pressure decreases with height; so the lower the air pressure, the higher the aircraft.

In the cockpit of an aeroplane

Refuelling an aeroplane in mid-air

What is the electronic altitude director indicator (EADI)?

The EADI is a flight instrument that tells the pilot whether the aeroplane is flying level. It is a round dial indicating the angle at which the aeroplane is flying. There are small lines, or bars, for depicting the position of the aeroplane with respect to the ground and the horizon.

Who was Charles Edward Taylor?

Charles Edward Taylor (1869-1956) was the world's first aeroplane mechanic. Taylor took about six weeks to build the engine for the Wright *Flyer*.

How are autopilots used on short flights?

Autopilots play a limited but important role on short flights. Besides helping the pilot to fly the aeroplane, they also run frequent checks during the flight to ensure that all the systems are working properly.

Do aeroplanes have speed indicators?

The air speed indicator (ASI) in the cockpit shows the speed in terms of knots (1 knot = 1.85 km/h) and the Mach number. Information about the aeroplane's speed through the air is fed to the ASI from a sensor called the pitot tube, fitted outside the aircraft.

FLIGHT RECORDER DO NOT OPEN

FACT BOX

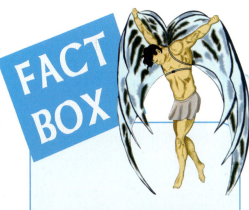

□ The first person to fly an aircraft at supersonic speed was Charles Yeager. In October 1947, the World War II pilot broke the sound barrier with the *Bell X-1*.

□ The autopilot was invented by Lawrence Sperry. He also invented other flight instruments, besides the aerial torpedo weapon and the parachute pack that pilots use in emergencies.

□ Aeroplanes are fitted with a fire-and-crash-proof flight data recorder. This recorder, called the black box, is red in colour and records everything that happens to the aircraft's main systems. It even records the conversations between members of the flight crew.

The black box helps to investigate what went wrong in an accident

AIRCRAFT TECHNOLOGY

Is a flight engineer part of an aeroplane's flight crew?

Flight engineers used to be part of the flight crew in the past (the first flight engineer on-board was Charley Furnas). Most modern airliners have a two-member crew, comprising the captain (pilot) and the co-pilot. The systems that were earlier managed by the flight engineer are now monitored by electronic equipment.

How do flight simulators recreate the runway, the clouds and other scenery outside the aircraft?

Scenes from real airports are projected on to a screen outside the cockpit window. This lets pilots practice take-offs and landings in 'real' conditions. For a realistic effect, aircraft sounds are fed through loudspeakers inside the simulator.

A vital member of the aircrew - the pilot

What are flight simulators?

Flight simulators are machines used for training pilots to fly new types of aircraft and to practice flying skills, including what to do in an emergency. These machines look like giant computer games. They are very popular as they save fuel costs and, of course, it is much safer to train on the ground than in the air.

Do flight simulators use electronic equipments similar to those in the cockpit of an aeroplane?

A flight simulator has the same flight deck as an aeroplane, complete with all the electronic controls. While trainee pilots manage the controls, an instructor sits behind them at all times for guidance. There are different simulators for different types of aeroplanes.

How do pilots experience the tilting and turning of an aeroplane while sitting in a flight simulator?

A flight simulator has legs that move to tilt in all directions. While the simulator is actually fixed to the ground, it is capable of tilting. This feature lets the pilot inside feel as though he is flying through air.

ON A FLIGHT

Passengers of modern air travel are treated to all kinds of on-board comforts - movies, music, telephone and email facilities, shopping, interesting menus, personal attention and spacious seats.

Aircraft Attendants

Flight attendants did not appear until the late 1920s, when some airliners hired male assistants. Called flight companions, cabin boys, or stewards, they attended to luggage and helped nervous passengers relax.

In 1930, Boeing introduced the first female flight attendants. They served passengers with sandwiches and water and chewing gum to help ease blocked ears!

The Jet Age

The advent of commercial jets brought about higher standards of technology and comfort. Trained ground staff and aircrew were introduced. In the mid-1930s, Douglas planes came with soundproof cabins, upholstered seats and padded armrests.

Passengers can now choose from the different classes of comfort offered by almost every airline.

Nowadays, sleeper seats with personal TVs and headphones provide home-like comfort to passengers

ON A FLIGHT

When did telephone service first feature on a flight?

In 1984, Airfone launched the world's first in-flight telephone system. The service was introduced on American Airlines aircraft. Today, over 4,000 aircraft have in-flight telephone services.

How are the life jackets on-board an aircraft helpful in an emergency?

Each passenger seat has a life jacket tucked under it. During emergency landings at sea, passengers put on a life jacket before exiting the aircraft. Once outside, they pull the toggle on the jackets to fill them with air. The air-filled jackets keep the passengers afloat on water.

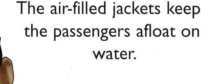

An air hostess explains how to use life jackets

How do escape chutes help in transporting passengers to safety?

Escape chutes are slide-like, inclined ramps made of lightweight material. In an emergency landing, chutes are inflated at the exit doors. Passengers slide down the chutes to the ground. At sea, they may be folded and used as life rafts.

Why are oxygen masks kept in the passenger cabin of an airliner?

Air pressure decreases with height above ground level. The air in the passenger cabin is artificially pressurised to maintain the same air pressure as that on the ground. If, however, the cabin air pressure falls, oxygen masks drop down to allow people to breathe safely.

Air hostess shows passengers how to use the oxygen mask

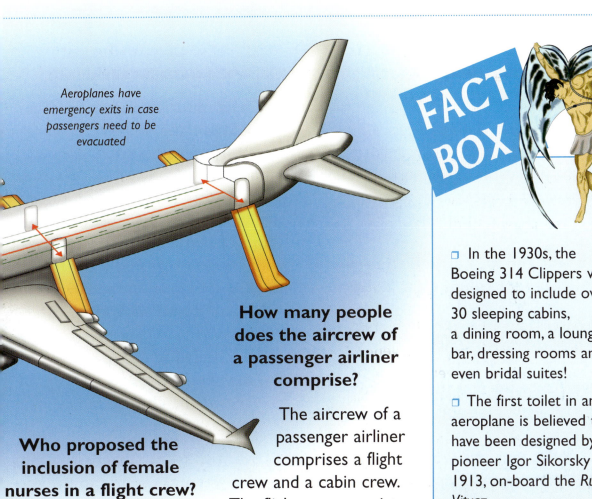

Aeroplanes have emergency exits in case passengers need to be evacuated

Who proposed the inclusion of female nurses in a flight crew?

In 1930, Ellen Church, a nurse, suggested that nurses be included in a flight crew for attending to sick passengers. Boeing promptly hired eight nurses for its crew. However, it is no longer compulsory for air hostesses to have a degree in nursing.

When was a movie first shown during a flight?

The first time a film was shown on-board a flight was in 1925. It was a silent, black-and-white movie titled *The Lost World*. The aeroplane was a converted World War I bomber.

How many people does the aircrew of a passenger airliner comprise?

The aircrew of a passenger airliner comprises a flight crew and a cabin crew. The flight crew consists of a pilot and a co-pilot. They sit in the cockpit and fly the plane. The cabin crew comprises a host of flight attendants and pursers who look after the comfort of passengers. They also help the passengers to leave the aircraft quickly and safely in an emergency.

FACT BOX

❑ In the 1930s, the Boeing 314 Clippers were designed to include over 30 sleeping cabins, a dining room, a lounge, a bar, dressing rooms and even bridal suites!

❑ The first toilet in an aeroplane is believed to have been designed by pioneer Igor Sikorsky in 1913, on-board the *Russky Vityaz*.

❑ The first in-flight meal was served in 1919, on a flight from London to Paris. The meal was said to include cream teas and cooked game. Food served during a flight is kept cool on trolleys with dry ice. This helps to keep the food fresh.

ON A FLIGHT

Which airline was the first to hire a fashion designer for flight attendant uniforms?

In 1965, Braniff Airlines hired fashion stylist Emilio Pucci to design uniforms for its flight attendants. The American airline was also the first to train women as airline mechanics.

Which was the first airline to serve freshly brewed coffee on a flight?

Trans World Airlines was the first to serve freshly brewed coffee on-board a flight. The New York-based airline is also believed to be the first to introduce a special section for non-smokers.

Who was the world's first air-crash victim?

On September 17, 1908, Thomas Selfridge became the world's first air-crash victim as the Wright *Model A* crashed at Fort Myer, Virginia. Selfridge was a passenger on the plane, which was being piloted by Orville Wright. While Orville survived the crash, Selfridge died on the spot.

Has Concorde ever had a major accident?

Concorde, the fastest passenger aeroplane in the world, faced its first major accident nearly 30 years after its first flight. On July 25, 2000, an Air France Concorde crashed shortly after take-off. It was suspected that a thin metal strip blew one of its tyres, which in turn ruptured the fuel tanks, causing the crash. All the 109 people on-board were killed.

Which airline company was the first to introduce a range of menus to choose from?

Virgin Atlantic was the first airline to offer over two types of meals to choose from. It was also the first to put videos on the back of every seat, on each one of their aeroplanes!

Thomas Selfridge did not survive the crash of the Wright Flyer

SHAPES IN THE SKY

From balloons and airships to modern aeroplanes, there have been several experiments in aircraft design. How has the shape and design of aircraft changed over time?

Strange Shapes!

The earliest flying machines were strange to look at. The first successful airship, built in 1852, was shaped like a cigar. Later, Leonard Bonney made a seagull-like aeroplane.

The unusual shape of the Lockheed F-114A keeps it from detection by enemy radars. Popularly called the Stealth Fighter, it was designed in the 1970s. More recently, in 1984, the Rutan Voyager was built in an H-shaped design.

The Rutan Voyager was the first to make a non-stop flight around the world without being refuelled

Science of Shapes

Aircraft design is based on aerodynamics. The shape of the fuselage can reduce drag and weight, or increase lift and thrust. Today, computers help people to design aircraft in the most favourable shapes.

However, an efficient and safe design is useless unless it is practicable. For instance, passenger airliners like the Boeing 747 also have to be spacious, with room for passengers and cargo.

Leonardo da Vinci's sketch of a flying machine

Which is the world's largest international airport?

King Khalid International Airport is the world's largest international airport. Located outside Riyadh, the royal capital of Saudi Arabia, the airport covers an area of about 223 sq km (86 square miles) and is worth some $2,625 million. Opened for public use on November 14, 1983, it has the world's largest control tower as well.

Where was aerial crop-dusting first carried out?

Crop-dusting - the process of spraying fertilizer, insecticide or fungicide (in powdered form) on crops from an aircraft - was first carried out in Ohio, U.S., in 1921. Lt. John B. Macready sprayed some insecticide from a Curtiss JN-6 light aircraft in order to treat an insect-infested grove.

Which famous painter studied the flight of birds and sketched the basic design of an aeroplane?

Leonardo da Vinci (1452-1519), the great Italian artist known for his masterpiece *Mona Lisa*, was one of the first people to dream of flight. He was so fascinated with the idea that he sketched plans for all sorts of flying machines. He studied the flight of bats and birds and came up with designs for an ornithopter, or flapping-wing aircraft.

What is the Codex Hammer?

The Codex Hammer is one of the notebooks of Leonardo da Vinci containing his scientific drawings. In 1994, it was acquired by the American billionaire, Bill Gates (founder of Microsoft), for $30,800,000 at an auction at Christie's in New York.

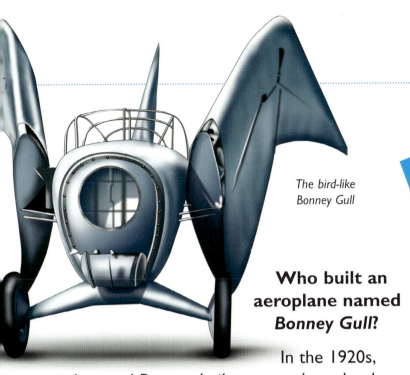

The bird-like Bonney Gull

Who built an aeroplane named *Bonney Gull*?

In the 1920s, Leonard Bonney built an aeroplane that he named *Bonney Gull*. He named it so because he had modelled it on seagulls!

Special aircraft are designed to carry out crop-dusting

What was the profession of Orville and Wilbur Wright before they began designing aircraft and became famous?

The Wright brothers were bicycle mechanics before they began designing aircraft. Their first successful glider went on some 1,000 flights. Later, they built the *Flyer*, the earliest heavier-than-air, powered aircraft. Orville Wright took the *Flyer* on its first, 12-second-long flight in 1903.

Which is the fastest aircraft in the world?

The North American X-15 is the fastest aircraft in the world. In 1967, it reached a speed of Mach 6.72, which is over six times the speed of sound. The X-15 does not have a jet engine. It is powered by a rocket.

FACT BOX

Icarus

❑ Icarus, the son of Daedalus, attached wax wings to his body and flew too close to the sun. His wings melted and he fell to his death in the sea. This legend is said to be about 2,000 years old and has become a symbol of impractical ambition.

❑ The Wright Brothers' *Vin Fiz* was the first aircraft to cross the North American continent. It was also the first to have an advertising message on it. Since the trip was being sponsored by the Armour Meat Packing Company, the plane carried a message for the company's grape drink below its wings!

❑ Tibet's Bangdag Airport, at about 4,300 metres (14,107 feet) above sea level, is the world's highest airport. It cost some $29.6 million to build.

SHAPES IN THE SKY

Concorde is the fastest passenger plane in the world

Is aeroplane racing a recognised sport?

Aeroplane racing, although not as popular as car racing, is a recognised sport. Fat, short aeroplanes called Gee Bees take part in these races. Balloon races were very popular before the invention of the aeroplane. The world's first international balloon race was held in 1906 in France.

The Lockheed SR-71 Blackbird

What is special about the Lockheed SR-71 Blackbird?

The Lockheed SR-71 Blackbird is the world's fastest aircraft driven by a jet engine. This U.S. spy aircraft touched Mach 3.3 in 1976. It is no longer in military service, but is now used for scientific research into the upper layers of the atmosphere.

Which is the world's fastest and only supersonic passenger airliner?

Concorde, which can travel at more than twice the speed of sound, is the world's fastest and only supersonic airliner. Jointly developed by Britain and France, Concorde was first flown in 1969 and is due to have its last scheduled flight in 2003..

What is the *Spruce Goose*?

The American flying boat, *Spruce Goose*, is the largest aircraft ever to have been built. This 55 metre (181 foot) long boat was built in 1947 from laminated birch wood. It was piloted by an American millionaire, Howard Hughes, on its one and only flight. The *Spruce Goose* got its name after its huge size made it impossible to use! It is now a part of the Evergreen International Aviation Museum, Oregon.

How long did the first non-stop, around-the-world flight last?

The fist non-stop, around-the-world flight lasted exactly 94 hours and 1 minute. Captain James Gallagher and his crew achieved the feat in the year 1948, in a Boeing B-50A Superfortress. Taking off from Fort Worth, Texas, the aircraft was refuelled four times in mid-flight.

HELICOPTER HIGHS

Among the many innovations in aircraft, the helicopter particularly stands out. Moving in ways that no aeroplane can, the helicopter is considered to be the most versatile flying machine.

The forces that work on an aeroplane – lift, weight, thrust and drag – also work on a helicopter. So what makes the helicopter more adaptable? What enables it to fly backwards and hover in air without moving?

Copter Components

Helicopters come in many different types, but they all share certain basic features.

The most important component of a helicopter is the main rotor, or propeller. The propeller's blades, situated above the fuselage, provide the helicopter with lift as well as the means to move forward, backward and sideways. The helicopter usually has a tail boom jutting out at the back, at the end of which is the tail rotor. This keeps the helicopter from spinning around while the main rotor is still running. It also lets the pilot steer the helicopter through left and right directions.

A helicopter's rotors can continue rotating even after a power failure. As the helicopter descends, the force of air over the blades keeps the rotors propelling. This gives the helicopter enough lift to have a controlled landing.

HELICOPTER HIGHS

A rescue helicopter of the Red Cross

Who was Louis Breguet?

Louis Breguet was a French designer who, in 1907, designed the first helicopter to be flown by a pilot. Breguet was airborne for one minute, while his helpers kept the helicopter in place with ropes, so that it would not fly away!

When was the first known flying helicopter invented?

The earliest known flying helicopter was built in 1784 by two Frenchmen, Launoy and Bienvenu. They fixed two rotors, made of turkey feathers, on the tips of a pole. A spring fixed between the rotors caused the rotors to propel for a few seconds, sending the 'helicopter' spinning. The Frenchmen had based their design on the Chinese spinning top!

What was the duration of the first flight made by the VS-300 helicopter?

On its very first flight in 1941, the VS-300 set a world record for helicopters, by flying for 1 hour and 33 minutes.

How are helicopters handy in emergencies?

Helicopters can reach places inaccessible to road vehicles and in which aeroplanes cannot land. They can avoid traffic and attend to emergencies quicker than ambulances. The ability to hover in mid-air allows helicopters to rescue people by lowering stretchers or harnesses on to the ground. Some rescue helicopters even have equipment that helps locate people in the dark by their body heat!

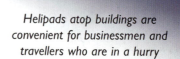

Helipads atop buildings are convenient for businessmen and travellers who are in a hurry

Who built the 'Flying Bicycle'?

In 1907, Paul Cornu, a French bicycle maker, invented a helicopter that had two rotors fixed on to bicycle-like wheels. It stayed in the air for about 20 seconds. To stop it from flying off in another direction, men on the ground are said to have held it in place with sticks!

Which was the first single-propeller helicopter?

The Sikorsky VS-300 was the world's first single-rotor helicopter. The aircraft was designed by Igor Sikorsky in 1940. Deployed during World War II by British and American forces, it also became the first helicopter to be used for military purposes.

What is a helipad?

A helipad is a landing place for a helicopter. It is quite common to find one at hospitals and office towers, since it helps patients and business professionals save time . Such helipads are usually located on the rooftops of buildings.

FACT BOX

□ The first president to use a helicopter was Dwight D. Eisenhower. The lawns of the White House served as a helipad. Eisenhower was also the first president to have a pilot's licence!

□ The first female pilot to fly around the world in a helicopter was Jennifer Murray from England. The 57-year-old flew a total distance of about 57,449 km (35,698 miles) in a Robinson R44 Astro. The trip took 97 days.

□ Igor Sikorsky is regarded as the 'Father of Helicopters'. Although he did not invent the very first helicopter, he built the first successful one, setting the standards for future designs.

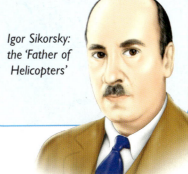

Igor Sikorsky: the 'Father of Helicopters'

HELICOPTER HIGHS

What is unique about the CarterCopter?

The CarterCopter is a gyroplane that features both a rotor and a fixed wing. During take-off, the rotor provides the aircraft with lift, as for regular helicopters. Once the CarterCopter gains height and speed, its fixed wing provides for a steady increase in lift, as is the case in fixed-wing aeroplanes. The CarterCopter's propeller is fully computerised and lightweight.

The CarterCopter

What can a helicopter do that an aeroplane cannot?

Unlike an aeroplane, the helicopter can fly backwards, hover in the air without moving and even rotate in mid-air!

What does the word 'helicopter' mean?

The word 'helicopter' comes from Greek terms - *helix*, which means 'spiral', and *pteron*, meaning 'wing'.

Which aircraft combines the features of both a helicopter and an aeroplane?

A hovercraft is part-helicopter, part-aeroplane. It is often called an amphibious vehicle. Invented in 1955 by Christopher Cockerell, a British engineer, the hovercraft has a helicopter-like rotor that carries it into the air and a jet engine that helps it sustain the flight.

What role do helicopters play in the world of television and cinema?

Helicopters are one of the most popular means of aerial filming. They are used extensively by television and cinema crews in shooting. Nowadays, aerial filming services are common all over the world. Hi-tech helicopters come ready with fixed cameras and other sophisticated filming gadgets.

Aerial filming has become easier thanks to helicopters with inbuilt cameras and filming equiments